The Social Market Foundation

The Foundation's main ac⸍⸍⸍
publish original pa⸍   r
experts on key topi⸍
a view to stimulatin⸍   ⸍f
markets and the socia⸍   ⸍⸍ace.
The Foundation is a re⸍   ⸍⸍pany limited
by guarantee. It is inde⸍   ⸍ political party or group
and is financed by the sa⸍   ⸍ublications and by voluntary
donations from individuals, organisations and companies.
The views expressed in publications are those of the authors
and do not represent a corporate opinion of the Foundation.

Chairman
David Lipsey (Lord Lipsey of Tooting Bec)

Members of the Board
Viscount Chandos
Gavyn Davies
David Edmonds
John McFadden
Brian Pomeroy

Acting Director
Ann Rossiter

First published by
The Social Market Foundation,
June 2005

The Social Market Foundation
11 Tufton Street
London SW1P 3QB

Designed by Paula Snell Design

This report is the product of a Commission conducted internally within the Social Market Foundation, and consisting of staff members. The members of the Commission were as follows:

Vidhya Alakeson
Jessica Asato
Philip Collins
Robin Harding
Moussa Haddad (Secretary)
Niall Maclean
Ann Rossiter (Chair)
Claudia Wood

Contents

Preface

Incapacity Benefit (IB) is a vital safety net for all those with a health condition that contributes to their inability to work. Yet, while it might be appropriate for those who cannot realistically expect to work again, it may not be serving the best interests of those who harbour hopes of working in the future.

Whatever reforms are made to the benefit in the Government's forthcoming White Paper must serve two distinct objectives. First, they must ensure that the state continues to provide a safety net and a decent standard of living to those who cannot reasonably be expected to work again in the future. Second, the state should do more to support individuals back into work who have a medical condition that has contributed to their unemployment, while providing them with financial support during their time out of work.

What is lacking is a class of benefit specifically tailored to the unemployed sick, giving them not just regular job-seeking support, but also the additional support that those with illnesses require. Until the state recognises the particular needs of these individuals and the barriers to their employment on both the demand and supply sides, the employment rate for the sick and disabled in the UK will remain shamefully low, with millions caught in what has become an incapacity trap.

1. Introduction

There are more than 2.7 million claimants of Incapacity Benefit (IB) and Severe Disablement Allowance (SDA) in the UK (the latter having effectively become part of the same category in April 2001 when claims were ended and would-be claimants directed to Incapacity Benefit instead).[1] The number of claimants of these benefits is quadruple the number (690,000) claiming equivalent benefits in 1979, despite no worsening of health and sickness during the period, although growing recognition of mental illnesses has made some contribution to the rise. In the past decade, the number of claimants has barely altered, in spite of a strong economy that has dramatically lowered unemployment. In May 1995, there were 2.75 million people on IB and SDA and 2.47 million unemployed (Labour Force Survey Measure); in May 2004, there were 2.71 million people on IB and SDA and 1.43 million unemployed.

There is much to suggest that the large numbers on incapacity-related benefits represent an unemployment problem and not one of overwhelming levels of disability. IB claimants are concentrated in the less affluent regions of the UK. As a national average, 6.8 percent of the working population claim Incapacity Benefit. This figure rises to 11.2 percent in Wales, 10.6 percent in the North East, 9.6 percent in the North West and 9.2 percent in Scotland, but only 3.8 percent in the South East, 4.3 percent in the Eastern region, 5.2 percent in the South West and 5.6 percent in London. The common impression that IB receipt is highest in areas suffering from the decline of heavy industries is reinforced by looking at the level of claims by district. Around half of the 20 districts with the highest proportion of male sickness claimants are either former coalmining areas or areas which relied upon the steel and shipbuilding industries. In the colliery towns of Merthyr Tydfil in

1 DWP figures May 2004: 2,708,700 in total, of which 2,404,900 on Incapacity Benefit and 303,800 on Severe Disablement Allowance "http://www.dwp.gov.uk/asd/asd1/ib_sda/ib_sda_may04_%20rounded.xls"

2 Paragraph 15, Fourth Report of the House of Commons Work and Pensions Select Committee, Session 2002-03, 2 April 2003

3 *Incapacity Benefit and Unemployment*, C. Beatty, S. Fothergill, 1999, Centre for Regional Economic and Social Research, Sheffield Hallam University, Sheffield.

4 Beatty et al. (1997)

5 Turok & Edge (1999), Bailey & Turok (2000)

6 Fieldhouse & Hollywood (1999)

7 *New Deal for Disabled People: National Survey of incapacity benefits claimants*, Research Report No. 160, By Julia Loumidis, Rachel Youngs, Carli Lessof and Bruce Stafford

8 EU Statistical Office (Eurostat)

9 *Fraud and Error in Claims to Incapacity Benefit: The Results of the Benefit Review of Incapacity Benefit*, Department for Work and Pensions Analytical Services Division, 2001

10 *Fraud and Error in Jobseeker's Allowance from April 2002 to March 2003*, Department for Work and Pensions Information and Analysis Directorate, 2004

South Wales and Easington in County Durham, more than a quarter of men aged 16-64 are in receipt of IB or Disability Living Allowance (DLA). The House of Commons Work and Pensions Select Committee concluded that the state of the local labour market has a strong effect on the likelihood of disabled people working, and that if that local labour market is buoyant, more disabled people will move into work.[2]

That sickness is not the only driver behind increases in IB claims is borne out by a study by the Centre for Regional Economic and Social Research at Sheffield Hallam University. It found that 53 percent of those on IB had left work for reasons unrelated to health.[3] Recent studies of the labour market in coalfields,[4] industrial cities[5] and for coalminers[6] have shown that for a high proportion of people affected by job losses, the consequence is not unemployment but other forms of economic inactivity, often sickness. Analysis based on the Labour Force Survey (LFS) showed that the propensity of the unemployed to move into inactivity rose steadily during the 1990s, from about 8 percent to 13 percent per quarter. A Department for Work and Pensions (DWP) survey found that 58 percent of incapacity-related benefit claimants did not think their health was a major barrier to work.[7]

The proportion of the working age population in the UK claiming disability benefits is high when compared internationally, whereas the proportion as a whole out of work is similar. In 1999, figures showed economic inactivity due to sickness or disability in the UK to be the highest in the entire European Union (EU). Despite enjoying one of the EU's lowest rates of International Labour Organisation (ILO) unemployment, the same year's figures show that only Spain and Finland fare worse than the UK when unemployment and inactivity due to sickness or disability are combined. Britain is one of only four countries in the EU in which the proportion of people inactive due to sickness or disability is greater than the proportion unemployed; in most, it is less than half.[8] None of this is to suggest, however, that IB figures are a reflection of people claiming the benefit wrongly or fraudulently. The DWP's own study concluded that IB has a fraud level of less than 0.5 percent,[9] which compares favourably with the numbers for Jobseeker's Allowance (6 percent) and Income Support (3.6 percent).[10]

Incapacity Benefit quickly breeds a culture of dependency, a problem which is worsening. Today, more than half of those claiming IB have received it for five years or more – a figure that was only 46 percent in November 2000 and has risen steadily since. Only 16 percent claim for a year or less. Once a claimant has been on IB for a year, his chances of ever getting off it are slim, with an average duration of eight years on the benefit.[11] To take the example of sickness absence due to back pain, after six months' absence due to this ailment, there is about a 50 percent chance of returning to work. This return-to-work rate falls to 25 percent after one year and 10 percent after two. Few individuals ever return to work after two years, irrespective of further treatment.[12] The longevity of IB claims contrasts with those claiming benefits for unemployment, with only 5 percent of claims lasting five years or more.[13]

On the positive side, the number of new claims is falling: from a peak of almost a million in 1994/5, the number of new claims for incapacity related benefits has fallen steadily each year, to around 610,000 in 2001/02. Unfortunately, of the 104,700 people who left IB in the quarter to February 2004, more did so because they died (6,700 – 6.4 percent of those leaving IB) than because of a return to work (5,200 – 5.0 percent), with the remainder moving on to other benefits. Also, while new claims have decreased, the caseload continues to rise (albeit slowly), as people are staying longer on the benefit. This reflects an age distribution that sees 35.7 percent of claimants aged 50-59, 12.7 percent aged 60 or over and only 6.5 percent aged under 25.

11 Paragraph 4, Fourth Report of the Work and Pensions Select Committee, Session 2002-03, 2 April 2003

12 Speech by Rosie Winterton MP, Minister of State, 11th February 2004: 'NHS perspective of the incapacity benefit reforms'

13 *Pathways to Work: Helping people into employment*, November 2002, Department for Work and Pensions

2. Problems with Incapacity Benefit

14 Paragraph 19, Fourth
Report of the House of
Commons Work and Pensions
Select Committee, Session
2002-03, 2 April 2003

15 *Pathways to Work: Helping
people into employment*,
November 2002, Department
for Work and Pensions

16 *Defending Incapacity
Benefit*, Trade Unions Congress,
7th October 2004

17 *The Future of Incapacity
Benefit*, Report of the Social
Market Foundation seminar
December 2004 ed. Haddad,
M., February 2005

A fundamental problem with IB is that it is a one-size-fits-all benefit that classifies each of its 2.4 million claimants as equally incapable of work. The single, binary test of incapacity is clearly flawed: people are classed as either incapacitated or not. This ignores the existence of a spectrum of incapacity, in which people may be capable of certain types of work and not others, or capable of working only given certain conditions. Furthermore, the label of 'incapacitated', assigned to all those claiming IB, can be debilitating in itself, a conclusion reached by the House of Commons Work and Pensions Select Committee.[14] A DWP study in 2002 concluded that time spent out of work and claiming IB can both be detrimental to health and well-being and increase a person's distance from the labour market.[15] In spite of two-fifths of IB claimants saying that they want to work now and only 11 percent feeling they will be unable to work in the future,[16] only 3 percent of all IB claimants are taking active steps towards finding a job.[17]

2.1 Problems with Incapacity Benefit off-flows

To some extent, the problems of IB centre around getting people off the benefit more than preventing them from getting on it in the first place. Indeed, many factors that discourage people from leaving the benefit, such as its low conditionality or the relatively high level at which it is paid (both discussed below), also act to encourage people on to the benefit in the first place. Nevertheless, the 1995 reforms that replaced Invalidity Benefit and Sickness Benefit with IB focused on tightening the gateway to sickness related benefits through an apparently objective test on work capability, the Personal Capability Assessment (PCA), drawn up by a panel of experts from different fields and then verified by independent DWP doctors. To a certain extent, this can be said to have been successful: annual flows onto incapacity-related benefits have fallen by nearly a quarter since 1996 according to HM Treasury's 2003 Budget Report.[18] Yet the total number of claimants has barely shifted in the last decade, with people spending an increasingly long period of time on IB, notably the high proportion of claimants who fail to leave the benefit within the first year. This tells us two things: first, that it is desirable to help people avoid unnecessarily claiming sickness related benefits in the first place and to focus on as quick a return to work as possible; and second, that IB as it exists, and the support mechanisms around it, are not doing enough to help long-term claimants back into work.

Financial incentives for moving off IB are weak. Prior to the introduction of the Working Tax Credit, just 25 percent of incapacity benefit claimants would have been £40 a week better off in work (commonly cited as the critical threshold for encouraging people back into work), a proportion that has now risen to 50 percent.[19] Lack of information about tax credits might, however, undermine their effect in improving incentives. This is partly the reasoning behind the introduction in the Pathways to Work pilots of a straightforward Return to Work Credit of £40 per week for a year for those moving into employment from IB.

The sufferers of some conditions, in particular those who have mental health problems, often need a gradual reintroduction to employment through part-time work. In this case, incentives to return to work are weaker still. The Permitted Work rules in place since 2002 ostensibly go some way towards solving these problems and are welcome. But the upper threshold of 16 hours' minimum wage work per week is too limiting to be of use to all those requiring a staged return to work. (See section 3.3 for more information on the Permitted Work rules).

The fact that IB is not means-tested also skews incentives, particularly for the 50 percent of claimants who are over 50. IB has earned the epithet 'the poor man's pension' and there is an element of truth behind this. A study by Beatty and Fothergill[20] concluded that possession of an occupational pension was, for this demographic, a significant predictor of whether they make

18 See http://www.hm-treasury.gov.uk/budget/bud03/budget_report/bud_bud03_repchap4.cfm

19 *Pathways to Work: Helping people into employment*, November 2002, Department for Work and Pensions

20 *Incapacity Benefit and Unemployment*, Beatty, C. and Fothergill, S., 1999, Centre for Regional Economic and Social Research, Sheffield Hallam University

21 At the moment contribu-tion-based JSA is paid out at £55.65 for those aged 25 or over and long-term basic rate IB is paid out at £74.15.

22 House of Commons Committee of Public Accounts, Sixteenth report: progress in improving the medical assess-ment of incapacity and disability benefits (HC120)

an IB claim as opposed to a JSA claim. Since JSA is means tested it removes the benefit of the pension, whereas IB is non-means tested and, therefore, amenable to being used as a subsidy for early retirement.

Differences between IB and other major benefits, notably JSA, also act as an incentive to claim IB. Not only is the level at which IB is paid significantly higher,[21] but the relative levels of conditionality of the two benefits create a strong incentive to claim IB. Whereas demonstrating an active search for work is a condition of continued receipt of JSA, for IB there are no job seeking requirements placed upon claimants. Even in the Pathways to Work pilots, the requirements begin and end with compulsory attendance of work-focused interviews and do not extend to any action arising out of them. Indeed, to attach job search requirements to a benefit for which a condition of receipt is incapacity for any work would be somewhat incongruous.

The level of job-related contact that an IB claimant receives is minimal. After submission of the Personality Capability Assessment form, the average waiting period before contact with a DWP doctor is 30 days,[22] and even then the contact is limited to an appraisal of whether the PCA's conclusions are correct. Thereafter, the only official contact takes the form of follow-up assessments by DWP doctors, contact which is infrequent and sporadic. IB as a whole is insufficiently focused on an eventual return to work, a problem exacerbated by the binary distinction between the healthy and the incapacitated. Moreover, given that the prospects of gaining work once on IB are so slim, the various incentives detailed above that push those who are both disabled and unemployed in the direction of IB rather than JSA are detrimental to their future employment prospects. Again, the issue is not that people are claiming IB inappropriately, but that IB itself is inappropriate for many of the people claiming it.

There are other, non-financial barriers faced by those on IB in returning to work, which the present system could do more to address. In particular, according to a recent DWP survey, the most commonly cited barrier to work for those on IB was the risk of a relapse leading to them losing their entitlement to benefit. This is exacerbated both by the drawn-out process for new IB applications (see section 2.2 below) and the fact that benefit levels increase with length of time spent on IB,[23] a hangover from when the period of disability was used as a proxy for its severity. The more fundamental problem, however, is the inflexibility of the IB system where trying work is concerned. Permitted Work rules allow limited trials of work by IB claimants but there is a lack of awareness about these and, crucially, they limit work to 16 hours and £67.50 per week. Approval by a Job Broker, Disability Employment Adviser or Personal Adviser is required for any extension. While this might be helpful in a limited set of cases, it does not address the needs of those who are apprehensive about a return to full-time work.

Fear of prejudice in the workplace is also cited as a substantial barrier to work.[24] The Disability Discrimination Act (DDA) is designed to act as a counter to this, yet there is evidence to suggest that a significant number of people are nonetheless denied employment on the basis of their disability,[25] particularly those with a mental illness.[26] This is reflected in the fact that mentally-ill people are the least likely group of disabled people to be in employment – with a 21 percent employment rate compared with 47.9 percent on average for disabled people as a whole.[27] Only 4 out of 10 employers say they would recruit someone with a mental health problem.[28]

A further problem is that the requirement under the DDA for firms to make 'reasonable adjustments' to secure retention or recruitment of disabled people is affected by factors beyond the condition of the employee. What constitutes a reasonable adjustment in order to recruit or retain a disabled person is, broadly speaking, dependent on the scope and cost of the adjustment in question and on the resources of the employer.

Government support is available through Access to Work (AtW), described by the British Chamber of Commerce as 'the best kept secret in government'.

----

23 For the first 28 weeks of illness, individuals are paid either Statutory Sick Pay at £68.20 or Short-term Incapacity Benefit lower rate at £55.90 per week, followed for the next 24 weeks by Short-term Incapacity Benefit higher rate at £66.15, and thereafter by Long-term Incapacity Benefit at £74.15, with the latter having potential age additions of up to £15.55 See: http://www.dwp.gov.uk/publications/dwp/2004/gJ23_apr.pdf

24 See, for example, *Out of the Picture – CAB evidence on mental health and social exclusion*, Lesley Cullen, April 2004, Citizens' Advice Bureau

25 For example, *Employment of Disabled People: Assessing the Extent of Participation*, Meager, N., Bates, P., Dench, S., Honey, S. and Williams M., DfEE Research Report RR69, 1998 found that 16 percent of disabled people who are or have been economically active say that they have experienced discrimination or unfair treatment in a work-related context, with 83 percent saying this came from an employer or from a potential employer

26 See, for example, *Mental Health and Social Exclusion*, Citizens Advice Bureau, 2004

27 p.5 *Mental Health and Social Exclusion*, Social Exclusion Unit, May 2003; Labour market experiences of people with disabilities, Smith, A and Twomey, B, Labour Market Division, Office of National Statistics

28 *Mental Health and Social Exclusion*, Social Exclusion Unit report summary, May 2003

29 *Access to Work for disabled people*, Disability Employment Coalition, August 2004

30 *Work Matters 2 – Beyond the Stereotype*, Simkiss, P., Assistant Director, Employment, RNIB, June 2004

31 *Access to Work for Disabled People*, Disability Employment Coalition, August 2004

32 52 percent, Figure 9, Annex A, *Pathways to Work: Helping people into employment*, November 2002, Department for Work and Pensions

What this means in practice is in the process of being established by case law. Past judgments have so far focused on four elements: practicality, effectiveness, disruptiveness, and finance.

With respect to finance, the questions asked by the courts have been whether the company in question can afford the adjustment. This is largely dependent upon the cost of the adjustment relative to the size of the company and whether the company is being offered financial assistance by government or charitable organisations. Government support is available through Access to Work (AtW), described by the British Chamber of Commerce as 'the best kept secret in government'. AtW has been in operation since 1994 and is a Job Centre-administered scheme to provide assistance in meeting both the one-off and on-going costs of employing a disabled person. The scheme is widely supported; the Disability Employment Coalition praised AtW as it 'can fund a wide range of supports and a strength is its flexibility, providing scope for creative solutions'. But it suffers from a lack of funding. In 2003/4, its budget was capped at £50 million, meaning that not all who applied could expect to be funded, regardless of eligibility. This is despite the fact that for every £1 spent on AtW around £1.48 is recouped in tax and NI contributions.[29]

There are other problems with the scheme: only 74 percent of employers are aware of AtW, and an RNID survey found that more than half of deaf people seeking work were unaware of it.[30] The budget for advertising AtW is tiny, perhaps as little as £37,500 per year according to the Disability Employment Coalition.[31] It has also been beset by administrative difficulties, resulting in delays that in some instances have led to job offers being withdrawn. Moreover the process itself is complex: AtW must be applied for by a specific employer for a specific employee for a specific job, resulting in confusion that hinders disabled people's access to employment.

Many of those on IB face barriers to work in addition to those that are directly due to their disability. With the average duration of an IB claim standing at over five years, and with more than half[32] having been out of work for non-health related reasons prior to making a claim, a substantial proportion of IB claimants are long-term unemployed, as well as suffering from an illness or disability. Lack of skills is a significant barrier to re-employment: around half of claimants have no formal qualifications.[33] IB claims are concentrated in recently de-industrialised areas, and so many claimants require retraining in order to have better prospects of re-employment. Meanwhile, the likelihood of making an IB claim rises as average income falls. Yet, while New Deal programmes have been used extensively to support the long-term unemployed on JSA and Income Support back into employment, there is a clear unmet need with regard to those on IB.

Revealingly, according to the Strategy Unit, the proportion of economically inactive men with a health problem or disability who would like to work is higher than the proportion of those without a health problem or disability.[34] Although the New Deal for Disabled People (NDDP)[35] has been available nationwide since 2001, as of June 2004, only 99,260 people (out of a potential 2 million on incapacity benefit) had had an initial interview with an employment adviser. Of these, 70,860 went on to participate in a programme. In spite of the low levels of take up, the scheme has apparently been successful, with 45,390 people, or 64 percent of participants, having been placed into jobs.

The unmet need for personal advice is being tackled by the Government through the Personal Adviser element of the Pathways to Work pilots, in which new IB claimants must attend a total of seven work focused interviews which aim to link claimants into advice to help them overcome both health and non-health related barriers to employment. At present, however, these pilots operate in only eight Jobcentre Plus areas in England and Wales, and do not confront the more complex problems faced by those who have already been on IB for a substantial length of time. Nonetheless, we welcome the proposal to extend Pathways to Work to one third of the country by October 2005 and then nationwide.

The use of Personal Advisers also helps to remedy the failure of the existing strategy to co-ordinate support to move people off IB. The problems faced by IB claimants in re-entering the labour market are, as demonstrated above, complex and multifaceted. Support for those on IB, as presently constituted, is often disconnected and disjointed and does not focus sufficiently on a swift return to employment. The co-ordinating

33 Figure 2.18, *Improving the life chances of disabled people*, Burchardt, 2003, Prime Minister's Strategy Unit

34 *Improving the Life Chances of Disabled People*, Analytical Report, Prime Minister's Strategy Unit, June 2004

35 A voluntary programme of employment advice delivered through a network of Job Brokers, and in which those who have been on an incapacity related benefit for 28 weeks or more can participate.

36 Mental disorders account for 38 percent of claims, and musculoskeletal for 22 percent, *Pathways to Work: Helping people into employment*, November 2002, Department for Work and Pensions

37 Hiscock, J., and Ritchie, J. (September 2001) The Role of GP's in Sickness Certification (DWP Research Report No. 148) CDS

role of Personal Advisers is a welcome step towards a system that promotes holistic solutions that can overcome the multiple barriers the unemployed sick and disabled face in securing appropriate and sustainable employment.

2.2 Problems with Incapacity Benefit on-flows

Though the rate of IB claims is falling, there are nevertheless a number of significant issues surrounding the gateway to IB. Reaching an objective assessment is a particular problem. Experience both domestically and internationally suggests that there are two areas of difficulty. First, a number of conditions cannot be assessed without substantial reference to the subjective experiences of the patient. This is particularly applicable to many mental health and musculoskeletal problems, which together account for more than half of all IB claims.[36] Second, there will always be a degree of conflict between the need for an 'objective' medical assessment that attempts to limit itself as far as possible to interpreting a claimant's medical condition, without any reference to their personal circumstances, and the need for a medical understanding of the ongoing nature of a patient's condition in order to carry out an effective diagnosis. The latter necessitates some input from a doctor who has worked with the patient over an extended period.

This can place GPs in a difficult situation. Although the limit of a GP's obligations under the present system is to provide a synopsis of the medical condition of a patient who is submitting an IB claim, they can opt to provide additional supporting evidence for the claim. There is much anecdotal evidence of GPs feeling pressured to support their patients' IB claims to protect good doctor–patient relations. This is supported by a recent DWP survey on the role of GPs in sickness certification.[37] Many GPs may also be inclined to take a wider view of their responsibilities to their patients' welfare. Particularly in the case of mono-skill areas decimated by industrial decline and with few job opportunities, doctors may be reluctant, in the interests of their patients' welfare, to commit them to a long and fruitless search for work, particularly in the case of older patients. They may, therefore, be well-disposed to any IB claim patients may make.

The process of DWP doctors – the objective assessors – verifying IB claims is fraught with difficulties. First, there has historically been a significant backlog in processing claims, resulting in an average wait for this assessment of 30 days.[38] During this period IB is paid to all claimants. Not only does this cost a significant amount in benefits paid to those whose claims are ultimately refused, it also generates an extended period of uncertainty for valid claimants. Including a period on Statutory Sick Pay (SSP), many people have already been out of work for seven months by the time their claim for IB has been completed. This particular problem is being addressed. Additional resources have been allocated to reduce the backlog but there are no plans to produce a standard timescale for the processing of IB claims. There are currently significant regional variations in the length of time it takes for an appointment with a DWP doctor to be made.

There are also significant question marks over how accurately the independent assessments are carried out. Around 10 percent of claimants appeal after their IB examination.[39] Of these, 45 percent are upheld.[40] Such a large percentage hints at significant problems in attempting to reconcile a tough, objective gateway with fairness to all applicants so that no-one is inappropriately denied sickness related benefits. In addition to problems with the initial assessment, the review process for eligibility over time is ill defined, with the result that there are great inconsistencies in how often claimants have their status reviewed. Getting the review period right matters for two reasons: it is important to avoid testing where it is inappropriate, as it can cause considerable distress and humiliation to sick and disabled people; and it is vital that people whose conditions have improved sufficiently and can be expected to work should move off IB as quickly as is appropriate. This second reason takes on extra significance in view of the fact that, under the present system, the medical review is the only point in the cycle of their claim that those on IB are asked even to consider their future employment prospects.

38 House of Commons Committee of Public Accounts, Sixteenth report: progress in improving the medical assessment of incapacity and disability benefits (HC120). The wait has been reduced from a previous average of 52 days.

39 According to Citizens Advice, 520,000 IB examinations were carried out in 2002-2003 and 51,000 IB cases went to appeal. See http://www.citizensadvice.org.uk/index/campaigns/social_policy/parliamentary_briefings/pb_benefitsandtaxcredits/br_publics_account_committee

40 This is according to a sample of tribunal appeals carried out by the Appeals service. See *Report by the President of Appeal Tribunals on the Standards of Decision-making by the Secretary of State 2001-2002* http://www.appeals-service.gov.uk/901.htm

3. Reforms to Incapacity Benefit

41 *Department for Work and Pensions Five Year Strategy: Opportunity and Security Throughout Life*, February 2005

In reforming Incapacity Benefit, it is vital that we seek to break the specious link between sickness or disability and lack of employment that has served to make the large numbers on IB so intractable, despite progress in tackling the problems of other groups at a distance from the labour market. For this reason, the reforms set out in this report seek to put a return to work at the core of the system of benefits and support for the 90 percent of sick and disabled people coming onto IB who expect to work again. For those for whom a return to work is a realistic goal, we propose a new benefit, Rehabilitation Benefit, that explicitly tells its claimants that they *can* expect to work again and are *not* being written off. Meanwhile, Incapacity Benefit should continue to provide a vital safety net for those who cannot get back into work.

The distinction drawn by the Commission between those who can and cannot be expected to work in the future has since been adopted by the government. A new 'Rehabilitation Support Allowance' will apply to 'people with more manageable conditions' who can be expected to work, whereas those with more severe conditions will be eligible for 'Disability and Sickness Allowance' paid at a higher level.[41]

At the same time, we recognise that there are a range of problems that have caused the numbers on IB to remain so stubbornly high and that there is no one solution. Instead, we set out a holistic approach, designed to tackle all elements of the Incapacity Benefit problem. Individuals must be helped to be as work ready as possible, tackling not only their medical condition but also issues such as low skills, lack of confidence and financial disincentives to take employment. In addition, we must ensure that employers are willing and able to take on those with an illness or disability, so that there are jobs for those who want them. Recognising that the current 2.71 million claimants of IB and Severe Disablement Allowance are not a monolithic group, we must work to ensure that the support they receive is individually tailored to their needs. We set out below how this can be achieved through a combination of more sophisticated testing and personalised rehabilitation support.

3.1 Defining and testing sickness and disability

Definition of sickness and disability

As discussed in section 2, the term 'incapacity', as used to define eligibility for IB, groups together a diverse range of people with a range of different, sometimes overlapping, problems. Given the very low levels of fraud involved in IB,[42] however, we can make a general assertion that those on IB all share two characteristics: they are unemployed; and they have a health condition that has made a substantial contribution to their unemployment. The Disability Discrimination Act (DDA) defines a disabled person as being a person with 'a physical or mental impairment which has a substantial and long-term [meaning it has lasted, or is likely to last, for at least twelve months] adverse effect on his ability to carry out normal day-to-day activities'. While the DDA definition rightly includes those who are in work in spite of their condition, we can define some of those who are presently on IB as those who both satisfy the DDA definition of disability and are out of employment.

As we have identified, a fundamental problem of IB as presently constituted is that its definition stops there. Those with a disability or disabilities that lead to a certain degree of impairment (expressed by a certain score on the Personal Capability Assessment) and who are not employed, are simply labelled 'incapacitated'. Yet those on the incapacitated side of the binary can work/can't work distinction are themselves at differing levels of work-readiness. Within this group, there might be:

i.   those who cannot work at all at present but have an illness or disability with a quantifiable recovery schedule;

42 See section 1

43 *Work to welfare: how men became detached from the labour market*, Alcock, P., Beatty, C., Fothergill, S., Macmillan, R. and Yeandle, S., 2003, Cambridge University Press, Cambridge

ii. those who cannot work at present but may be able to at some point in the future;

iii. those who have an illness or disability that affects their ability to work at present, but who could nonetheless work in certain circumstances or conditions, in certain jobs or with certain support from employers;

iv. and those with a permanent disability which will prevent them from working again.

On this basis, we can create a new three-way distinction between:

i. those with no health problems preventing them from working (and who are therefore not eligible for IB);

ii. those with a health problem that prevents them from working in certain jobs or circumstances, but who we can, or will be reasonably able to, expect to work under certain conditions;

iii. and those who we cannot reasonably expect to work, now or in the future (which is still not to say that they cannot work under any circumstances, just that there should not be an expectation upon them to do so).

In testing for disability or sickness, we should seek to create a more nuanced definition than simply 'incapable of work', or even the DDA definition of having a health problem that poses substantial problems for everyday life, and by extension work. While there should still be a dividing line between those who suffer from health problems that have a substantial effect on their work and those who do not, our proposed replacement for IB, Rehabilitation Benefit, should be sophisticated enough to take account of the degree to which health problems affect a person's ability to work. The question should be closer to 'under what circumstances and in what types of employment can you work?' rather than 'can you work or not?'.

According to survey work from 2003, only a quarter of men claiming IB cannot do any work at all, despite them all having some form of work-limiting health problem or disability.[43]

Clearly, someone who has had to give up their normal profession because of a health problem is substantially disadvantaged by that problem, but it would be very crude to class him as incapable of all work as a result. Indeed, in Sweden, a person is defined as disabled only 'if the environment which they find themselves in is unable to properly accommodate their physical impairment'.[44] Hence, the DDA, in demanding that reasonable adjustments be made to ensure that people do not suffer disadvantage in employment, puts the responsibility in the first instance upon the employer. An accommodating workplace can make a significant contribution to avoiding disability leading to unemployment (see section 3.4 for more detail on the role of employers). An expansion of the Access to Work scheme should support a wider definition of what constitutes a 'reasonable adjustment'. Where adjustment proves impossible, it should then be up to the testing system to avoid an all-encompassing judgement of 'disability' and instead to concentrate on the areas in which someone with a health problem is able to work.

Finally, the judgement of sickness or disability should more explicitly include a judgement of anticipated recovery and regular reviews of status, both of which should depend on the condition in question. This will help to serve two key aims. Having regular reviews should keep the claimant focused on a return to work. Recognition that recovery is the expected outcome of a spell on benefit should help to break the link between disability and long-term incapacity. For those with a stable, long-term condition, condition-specific reviews will mean that unnecessary and intrusive re-testing can be avoided, with a focus instead on defining and exploring areas of capacity and capability for work.

44 Swedish Ministry of Health and Social affairs definition

Recognition that recovery is the expected outcome of a spell on benefit should help to break the link between disability and long-term incapacity

---

Testing for sickness and disability

The gateway

As is presently the case with IB, the decision to apply for our proposed Rehabilitation Benefit (RB) would arise where a work-inhibiting health problem is present, in one of two ways, depending on an individual's employment status. If an individual becomes ill while in regular employment, defined as having been in the same job for eight of the previous 21 weeks, he becomes eligible for Statutory Sick Pay (SSP) after the first four days of illness, paid by the employer at the rate of £68.20 per week (provided average gross earnings are more than £79.00 per week). It is only after 28 weeks on SSP that a claim for IB, or new RB, is made. Eligibility for SSP depends on a sick note from a medical professional, most probably the claimant's own GP, which need only demonstrate that the illness prevents the claimant from carrying out his normal occupation. If someone becomes ill when they are not in regular employment or when they are self-employed, they become eligible for IB at the short-term lower rate of £57.65 per week, as well as potential age-related additions. They must undergo an 'all work' assessment, as opposed to the 'own occupation test' given to those in regular employment (for proposed RB rates, see section 3.3). The difference in approach to the two groups of people reflects the desirability of those who are ill making a return to their original job or profession where possible.

As discussed earlier, there will be limits to the extent to which objectivity is pursued in assessing eligibility for RB. Given concerns about a potential conflict of interest between making medical judgements about eligibility for IB and maintaining doctor-patient relationships, however, there is a strong case for limiting the role of patients' own GPs in the assessment process for RB. Yet the medical professionals who have been involved in diagnosing and treating a patient's health condition throughout its duration are best placed to provide a medical assessment. The new assessment process for RB should, therefore, ask GPs and other medical professionals involved in diagnosis and treatment of their client's condition to provide a primary judgement of the nature of that condition and its general effects. The secondary judgement of the impact of the condition

on the claimant's likely employability should, however,
be entirely taken out of the hands of medical practitioners
involved in its treatment. The option in the IB system as it
currently stands for GPs to offer additional information in
support of a claim exposes them to direct or indirect pressure
from their patients and should be removed.

Instead, we propose that a judgement on the likely effect
of a claimant's medical condition on his employability should
be made by an independent medical expert, trained in the
process of administering RB tests. In the first instance, much
as at present, these should be GPs or former GPs who have
undergone special training in the administration of the tests.
The current number of doctors administering the tests – 200
full-time and 2000 part-time, usually GPs[45] – is insufficient and
causes excessive delays between making an IB claim and having
the claim accepted or refused. We would support a significant
increase in the number of doctors employed to carry out these
assessments. We are also in favour of simultaneously piloting
testing by specially trained Occupational Therapists, with a
view to the tests ultimately being carried out by qualified
Occupational Therapists, as in the Netherlands. By changing
the gatekeepers to IB/RB, we significantly change the gateway
because GPs will no longer be put under pressure to support
benefit claims in order to maintain professional relationships.
In this way, the system can maximise objectivity without losing
the detailed medical knowledge necessary for assessing
claimants' conditions.

The test

'Toughening up' or otherwise modifying the Personal
Capability Assessment (PCA) is a superficially attractive way
of reducing the numbers on incapacity-related benefits. Yet, as
discussed earlier, there is nothing to suggest mass defrauding of
the IB system: on the contrary, rates are lower than for JSA or
Income Support.[46] Most significantly, as highlighted in section
2.2, for a number of conditions, constituting a high proportion
of those leading to IB claims, no assessment can be made
without substantial reference to the subjective experience of
the patient. Moreover, in drawing up the PCA in 1995 a wide
range of experts and stakeholders were consulted and the test

45 According to Citizens Advice see: http://www.citizensadvice.org.uk/index/campaigns/social_policy/parliamentary_briefings/pb_benefitsandtaxcredits/br_publics_account_committee

46 See note 22

47 See section 2.1

48 The Netherlands social insurance disability benefits scheme.

devised to maximise objectivity.[47] International attempts at objective assessment have produced similar tests. For example, the medical element of the WAO test[48] in the Netherlands is remarkably similar in structure to the UK's PCA.

We therefore propose that the test for RB should function in the same way as at present for IB, up to the point at which the independent assessor determines whether or not someone has any work-inhibiting medical problem. This will entail using the claimant's PCA, their doctor's medical diagnosis and the assessment of a DWP doctor. The allocation of additional resources to fund extra assessors would reduce waiting times between application and assessment to two weeks. At this *work diagnosis* stage, all those with a health condition impacting substantially on their ability to work will be passed as eligible for one of two benefits – Incapacity Benefit and the new Rehabilitation Benefit. Those classed as ineligible for a sickness-related benefit will then be placed onto JSA.

For those eligible for either IB or RB, there will be a second judgement carried out by the same assessor. Using the GP's medical assessment and a set of clear guidelines and statistics on recovery prospects, an assessment can be made of whether the claimant can be reasonably expected to work in the future. The use of guidelines and statistics should maximise objectivity and keep appeals to a minimum. Those who we can expect to work in the future can then be placed on Rehabilitation Benefit, while those on whom we do not place such an expectation are placed on Incapacity Benefit. This can be classed as the *work prognosis* stage.

At this stage, the two groups – those designated for RB and those for IB – are treated differently. Those designated for IB are placed onto a benefit similar to the present IB, with no job-search related conditions. This benefit should be paid at the present higher rate of IB. It is currently payable after a year on IB and is used as a proxy for long-term incapacity. The assessor will, if appropriate, set a review period with a date for a follow-up test to consider future eligibility. If the illness or disability is such that there is no prospect whatsoever of recovery, then a review should not be ordered. All this is emphatically not to write off the employment prospects of those on the new IB. Rather, it is a recognition that their illness or disability is such that they cannot reasonably be expected to work and no steps should be taken to compel them to do so. There should still be a range of support available to those on IB to help them seek employment, including through the New Deal for Disabled People (see section 3.2) and through Access to Work (see section 3.4).

Those on RB are placed in a stream that emphasises a return to work. The first stage is to interpret the results of the test carried out through the PCA and the independent assessor. Using a system such as the Function Information System (FIS) in the Netherlands, a person's capabilities should be assessed against a database of the abilities required to perform different types of jobs. The FIS is a computer system which takes a representative sample of jobs, and for each job compares the physical and mental function required to perform it against the results of an earlier medical test of a claimant's capabilities, in order to assess whether the individual is prevented by their medical condition from doing that job. In the first instance, this information should be passed on to a Personal Adviser to help target the rehabilitation support package (see section 3.2). For a six month period following this initial assessment, no-one with a work-inhibiting ailment should be expected to take up work, though some degree of participation in a process of reha-bilitation should be compulsory. This should give those on RB a period of time to come to terms with their illness or disability and to receive the support of a trained specialist in helping them back into work, while not being under immediate pressure to take a job (see section 3.5 for more details on proposed conditionality).

After this six month period of rehabilitation with no job-search conditions imposed, RB claimants should have an automatic review of their status. (See section 3.2 for the need for a six month wait). This will lead to a second set of tests, following the same process as the initial tests, with a work diagnosis stage followed by a work prognosis stage and analysis of results through the FIS. The results produced by the FIS will provide a set of jobs which an RB claimant can reasonably be expected to do, given their illness or disability. It will be important for the test to recognise the needs of claimants with fluctuating conditions, for example by making part-time work

49 2-4 percent, according to NDDP take-up data

50 In a Department for Work and Pensions Press Release, 11th October 2004, Alan Johnson (Secretary of State for Work and Pensions) announced that success rates for people on IB getting into jobs were double in Pathways to Work areas compared with the national rate

or self-employment an option.

Once the second set of tests have taken place, given that claimants will have already received six months of rehabilitation support, RB should then be made conditional for those for whom it is appropriate. Conditionality should only apply to those who can be reasonably expected to work in some occupations now and not to those who we might expect to work in the future. For this latter group of RB claimants, the independent assessor will set a further review period to reassess their condition based upon the nature of the ailment and its likely progression.

Conditionality for those who can be reasonably expected to work in their current condition in some but not all occupations should be applied on the basis of capability. Instead of treating those with conditions that severely affect their ability to carry out day-to-day activities as incapacitated and those without such a condition as having a responsibility to work, we can use the FIS test to create a more nuanced set of responsibilities. The list of types of job produced by the FIS that a person is not prevented from doing by their ailment can be used as a way of defining the types of employment that a person can be reasonably expected to do. Given that all RB claimants are offered six months of holistic rehabilitation co-ordinated by their Personal Advisor (see section 3.2) prior to any conditionality being imposed, it is reasonable to expect them to take employment appropriate to their condition thereafter (see section 3.5 for further discussion of conditionality).

3.2 Rehabilitation support

The Commission welcomes the work already done giving IB claimants personalised support in job seeking through the Pathways to Work pilots. Given the extremely low proportion of IB claimants currently taking active steps towards seeking work,[49] having such steps co-ordinated through a single Personal Adviser is welcome. Although it is still too early for a definitive assessment of their success, initial signs from the pilots are encouraging. They have led to an increase in participation and in the chances of claimants gaining employment.[50] A word of caution is required, however. So far, the pilots have dealt with the 'easier' cases, namely those closer to employment, since they encompass only those coming onto IB, and not all existing claimants. Any expansion of Pathways to Work to include those who have already been on IB for some time will almost certainly mean a decrease in the average levels of success in getting people back into employment.

We therefore support the proposed expansion of Pathways to Work, both geographically to cover the entire country, and in terms of scope to cover all claimants of the new Rehabilitation Benefit (RB), both new and old. The support of a Personal Adviser should also be offered to those remaining on IB, though there will be no pressure placed upon them to accept, since they cannot reasonably be expected to work, now or in the foreseeable future. The role of the adviser should be to co-ordinate the rehabilitation support offered to claimants of RB, including the Condition Management Programmes (CMPs) offered through Pathways to Work itself. CMPs are six to thirteen week courses particularly aimed at those who have the three most common medical conditions among IB claimants: moderate mental health conditions, cardio-respiratory conditions and musculoskeletal conditions. They aim to help patients understand and manage their condition using 'cognitive behaviour therapy' based interventions and other validated techniques. This represents a welcome step towards making employment central to the rehabilitation process.

With strong evidence that IB is debilitating, there is a need for early intervention and so we would maintain a compulsory work-focused interview at the start of an RB claim, taking the same approach as Pathways to Work of scheduling the initial interview for eight weeks after the RB claim is made. This gap allows claimants to adjust to their illness. Work-focused interviews should continue at regular monthly intervals throughout the period of an RB claim, in order to ensure that a return to work remains a central goal.

Where in addition to the support offered in the CMPs a Personal Adviser believes that specific training is needed in order to promote an RB claimant's employment prospects, the client should be directed towards such training during the initial six month period of rehabilitation. Evidence from other New Deal programmes suggests that in-work training has the best success rate in getting people back into sustainable employment.[51]

51 *The New Deal for Young People: Effect of the options on the labour market status of young men*, Richard Dorsett, (London: Policy Studies Institute, 2004)

52 This should follow the example of the Pathways to Work pilots which provide In-Work Support (IWS). This may include support from a mentor, support from a job-coach, occupational health support, and more in-depth support

Personal Advisers should have the authority to offer employers a subsidy for up to 26 weeks to take on those on RB (see section 3.4 for more detail). An important element of the Personal Adviser's role will be simply to ensure that clients are aware of the range of support available to them. As well as the rehabilitation support, this will also include making them aware of financial incentives to work, such as the Return to Work Credit, and schemes that encourage participants to take the risk of returning to work, such as Permitted Work and the six month period during which all RB claimants may go back on benefit without sanction if they are unable to persevere with work (see section 3.3 for incentives for individuals to move into work).

As well as helping people from RB into work, Personal Advisers should also have a role in ensuring that people remain in employment once they have entered it. Those who enter employment from RB should automatically be offered support from their Personal Adviser for up to 26 weeks after taking a job. In this way, they can be helped to address any ongoing issues, medical or otherwise, they may have which might make it difficult for them to retain their job.[52] Where necessary, further rehabilitation support could be offered. In addition, existing personal advice available to those at risk of losing their job due to a medical condition through the New Deal for Disabled People should be better advertised and could be delivered by the same Personal Advisers that offer in-work support to those coming off RB.

Given that those coming on to RB will either have recently lost their job due to illness or disability, recently have become ill, or have spent a length of time on IB already, the rehabilitation process may take some time. For this reason, no-one on RB should be pressured to take a job during their first six months of rehabilitation support. In order to maintain a focus on a

---

Evidence from other New Deal programmes suggests that in-work training has the best success rate in getting people back into sustainable employment.

---

return to work, however, claimants should be compelled to attend a full series of work-focused interviews. Missing a work-focused interview without showing good cause to do so, which could include difficulties in keeping appointments due to an illness, such as depression, should result in a benefit cut, with separate cuts for each appointment missed.

3.3 Incentives for individuals to take work

If the role of rehabilitation support is to prepare IB claimants for returning to work, then the role of incentives is to encourage a group that might be apprehensive about working to take the risk of re-entering the labour market. To ensure that the risk of taking work is worthwhile for those with health conditions, there are two major principles that we should seek to support with the incentives. First, work should pay. Second, in addition to there being a positive incentive to seek work, incentives to take work should not be outweighed by the consequences of a failure to sustain work. Various sources cite fear of relapse as a major barrier to taking work for current IB claimants.[53] Reform must ensure that the financial impact of a failed attempt to return to sustained employment should not be so strong as to create an incentive to remain on benefits.

Payment levels

At present, those who are unable to work are, for their first six months of sickness or disability, either paid Statutory Sick Pay (SSP) at the rate of £66.15 per week or, if ineligible for SSP, the short-term lower rate of IB of £57.65 per week. For the second period of six months, this then rises to £68.20. Thereafter, IB is paid at the long-term basic rate of £76.45 per week. In addition, for those paid at the long-term rate, an Incapacity Age Addition is payable, depending upon the age of the claimant on their first day of incapacity: £8.05 for those aged 35-44 inclusive and £16.05 for those aged under 35. This rise in benefit in line with time spent on it creates decreasing incentives to seek work, entrenches benefit dependency, and discourages risk-taking behaviour with regard to job-seeking. If someone has been out of work on sickness-related benefits for over a year, any impulse they have to return to work must be tempered by the fact that, should they relapse, they will be

53 See, for example, *Out of the Picture – CAB evidence on mental health and social exclusion*, Lesley Cullen, April 2004, Citizens' Advice Bureau; and New Deal for Disabled People: National survey of incapacity benefits claimants, Loumidis, L., Youngs, R., Lessof, C. and Stafford, B., Research Report No. 160, Social Research Brance, Department for Work and Pensions, London.

54 Alan Johnson answer to oral question, House of Commons, Monday, 13 December 2004

forced to reclaim either SSP or the short-term lower rate of IB, leaving them between £10.30 and £34.85 a week worse off, depending on their age and the status of their employment. With the average duration of an IB claim for those who go on to claim the long-term rate standing at eight years,[54] there is a strong case for ending the increases in IB over time, thus removing a powerful disincentive for people to seek work.

Under the current system, the length of time spent on IB is seen as a proxy for the level of incapacity. While there is a case for suggesting that a more severe level of incapacity will tend to lead towards a longer claim, the duration of an ailment is nevertheless a crude way of measuring its severity. With the reforms to the assessment process outlined above (see section 3.1), our proposals offer a more sophisticated way of distinguishing between those who can be expected to seek work now or in the future and those who cannot. The former are placed onto the new Rehabilitation Benefit (RB) and the latter onto IB. We therefore propose that RB should be paid at the present short-term IB rate and IB at the long-term rate. This removes the incentive to stay on a disability benefit long-term where work is a realistic option, while continuing to compensate long-term disability where this is appropriate. Similarly, the age-related additions that afford extra compensation to younger IB claimants become unnecessary when we can instead compensate people on the basis of whether they can be reasonably expected to work again or not. Disability Living Allowance would continue to be available to deal with the specific costs associated with care and mobility. When combined with proactive rehabilitation support (see section 3.2), positive financial incentives to take work and greater freedom to try work (see below), ending the accelerator effect in IB payments will help to ensure that the financial incentives surrounding those with health problems are weighted firmly in favour of returning to work.

Financial incentives

Our proposed reforms to the levels at which RB is paid should in themselves substantially improve the financial incentive to take work. Meanwhile, the role of the minimum wage and tax credits in making work pay more broadly will, particularly in conjunction with the support of a Personal Adviser, help to increase the attractiveness of work once it is systematically presented as a realistic option.

At the same time, however, we have already recognised that those coming off IB (or its replacements) face additional barriers to employment, above and beyond those faced by other groups outside employment. A return-to-work credit is already in place in Pathways to Work areas. It is a non-taxable, flat rate payment of £40 per week for 12 months, offered to all those returning to work from IB (provided they work for more than 16 hours per week but earn under £15,000). The great virtue of this credit is its simplicity, but it also has a substantial effect on improving incentives. Being £40 per week better off is widely seen to be crucial in providing sufficient incentive for people to choose work over benefits, and the proportion of those coming off IB who cross this threshold increases from 25 percent to 50 percent through the return-to-work credit alone.[55] In the context of a framework of support and incentives that promote a return to work for the sick and disabled, we support retaining the return-to-work credit piloted through Pathways to Work and extending it nationally. It offers a clear reward and is a recognition that, for those with a health condition, there are extra difficulties associated with attempting a return to employment.

Dealing with fluctuating conditions and relapse
The section above deals with the first of our two considerations – making work pay. There remains, however, the significant issue

----

Being £40 per week better off is widely seen to be crucial in providing sufficient incentive for people to choose work over benefits and the proportion of those coming off IB who cross this threshold increases from 25 percent to 50 percent through the return-to-work credit alone.

----

56 *New Deal for Disabled People Evaluation, Eligible Population Survey Wave One, Interim Report*, Catherine Woodward, Anne Kazimirski, Andrew Shaw, Candice Pires, DWP, August 2003 http://www.dwp.gov.uk/jad/2003/170rep.pdf

of the fear of relapse. We have mentioned above the extent of the disincentive effect this produces but the facts bear repetition. In a DWP sponsored survey, half of IB claimants said that the possibility of returning to their original benefit if a return to work did not work out would have a major impact on their likelihood of taking work, making it the most commonly cited factor of all.[56]

Many of our proposed reforms to other areas of the IB system would work to lessen the extent to which fear of relapse acts as a barrier to seeking work. For example, breaking the link between levels of benefit and length of time spent on IB will remove the threat of reduced benefit in the future for those who return to work and later relapse. While these factors will serve to lessen the consequences of a failed attempt at returning to work, the threat of having to go through a reapplication process for sickness-related benefits would still act as a disincentive to job-seeking among those presently on IB. For those who wish to try small levels of work, the Permitted Work rules are a useful option but, at a maximum of 16 hours a week, they cannot hope to simulate the effect of a full-time return to work. Substantially increasing the number of hours that can be worked is not a viable option. Those undertaking Permitted Work are still entitled to full benefit and incentives to take full-time work as an alternative to benefits would be diminished by an extension of this kind. Instead, we propose treating those who take work but are forced to give up due to ill health as ill, and therefore entitled immediately to RB (or IB if they entered employment directly from that benefit). This will serve, in combination with financial incentives, to encourage people who are not sure whether they can work to make an attempt.

In order to prevent this entitlement generating incentives to leave work, we would propose a period of six months' employment during which an individual can return to their original benefit without penalty if their return to work does not work out. Those who relapse after a return to work can then be reconnected with rehabilitation support at the point at which they left it, having received post-employment support during their time in work.

Permitted Work, meanwhile, should continue to be offered to those for whom it is most appropriate, namely those whose condition demands that they are eased gradually back into work, and for whom a full time return to work is not presently appropriate. For this reason, Permitted Work should continue to be restricted on the basis of hours worked.

National Insurance contributions

Given that the primary rationale behind our proposals for reform is to ensure that all those with work-inhibiting sickness or disability receive the appropriate level of benefit, incentives to return to work and support package, RB and IB should no longer be contributions-based. They should instead be made available to all people equally, regardless of their work history. This should help to secure the necessary support for all sick and disabled individuals and particularly encourage people on those benefits to return to work.

3.4 The role of employers

The above reforms seek to counter the exclusion of those presently on Incapacity Benefit from the supply side active labour market policies that have been pursued with regard to, for example, the long-term unemployed.

Yet for groups such as the long-term unemployed who are at a disadvantage in the labour market, we recognise the extra risks, real or perceived, that employers face in taking on employees disadvantaged in the labour market. We have already outlined the multiple disadvantages that those on IB face. Many of these, such as a lack of qualifications or relevant work experience, are also common among groups such as the long-term unemployed. We therefore propose that Personal Advisers should have the option of offering incentives to employers on the same basis as those offered to employers taking on the long-term unemployed through the New Deal – with a maximum weekly subsidy of £70 per week. The maximum subsidy should be available only to those taking on people coming off a disability benefit who have also been long-term unemployed, with a lower premium offered where the RB claimant has not been long-term unemployed. This support can be seen as a premium to account for the risk encountered by employers in taking on those with a history of sickness or disability.

As under the New Deal, employers would be eligible for subsidies for a six month period. Limiting subsidies to the initial period of employment of a sick or disabled person should ensure that the risks of taking on such an employee are compensated, while preventing government subsidising over the long term workers who demonstrate low productivity.

As discussed in section 3.1, offering a risk premium to employers for taking on those who have been on IB (or RB) should be seen as a positive contribution to the rehabilitation of a group with multiple labour market disadvantages, since promoting in-work training has been demonstrated within the New Deal to be the best way of furthering the long-term employment prospects of disadvantaged groups.[57] Given that, as a group, present IB claimants are not identical to those eligible for New Deal for the long-term unemployed, the impact of this subsidy should be monitored, so that the level can be adjusted if it proves to be insufficient or excessive.

While subsidies for employers address the generalised risks of taking on those who have been on IB or RB, there will also be certain costs associated with employing sick or disabled individuals that are directly related to their sickness or disability. At present, the Disability Discrimination Act demands that such workplace adjustments as are necessary to overcome barriers to employing an individual caused by their sickness or disability be made, but only where it is 'reasonable' to do so. As discussed in section 2.1, a key determinant of whether an adjustment can be considered reasonable is the cost of that adjustment in relation to the size of the company concerned. Where a company cannot be expected to make an adjustment due to excessive cost, the existence of Government or charitable support becomes a determining factor.

The Access to Work scheme (AtW) has the potential to allow companies who otherwise could not adjust to an individual's disability to do so. Moreover, there is evidence to suggest a net benefit to the taxpayer as a result of money that is spent on the scheme.[58] Yet, as a result of its capped budget, inconsistent application and low awareness (see section 2.1), AtW currently pays for workplace adjustments on a fairly arbitrary basis. There is also a problem that larger companies are more likely than smaller employers to make adjustments to overcome barriers to recruitment or retention of disabled staff. Among larger companies (those employing 250 or more), 59 percent claim to have made such adjustments in recruitment and 88 percent in retention, compared to only 15 percent and 34 percent respectively among small and medium sized enterprises.[59] AtW could help to overcome this disparity by making it easier for smaller companies to make adjustments.

We would support an expansion of AtW so that it becomes an effective guarantee that adjustments will be made. To ensure that companies that are currently required to make adjustments for disabled people are not unnecessarily subsidised by AtW, the level of support available to a company should be dependent on its size. What is a reasonable adjustment for a company of a given size can be assessed through case law relating to the interpretation of the DDA. While AtW should be used to pay for both specific one-off adjustments and predictable longer-term support costs, the scheme should not be used to provide a long-term subsidy for low productivity. Any funding available through the scheme should be tied explicitly to the costs of adjusting a workplace to accommodate an employee with an illness or disability.

There is also a case for wider publicity of disability issues and the legal requirements pertaining to them among employers, particularly smaller employers. In a government survey, 73 percent of large businesses had a disability policy, either as a stand-alone policy or as part of a diversity policy. This figure fell to 45 percent among small and medium sized organisations, perhaps reflecting the fact that 90 percent of the former, but only 32 percent of the latter, claimed to employ disabled people.[60]

A more direct means of affecting the demand for the labour of disabled people is through sheltered employment. There is significant existing provision to this end in the UK, with Remploy employing 5,700 disabled people in 83 factories and its managed services division. There are groups for whom this is the most suitable model of employment, such as those with no realistic hope of re-entering the mainstream labour market, or those for whom a period of sheltered employment is judged the best means of easing back into work. Provision for these groups should remain in place but there is little to suggest that expanding this type of employment substantially is the right approach to take towards promoting sustainable employ-

59 *Small Employer Literature Review*, Marilyn Howard, (DRC, March 2004)

60 *The extent of use of health and safety requirements as a false excuse for not employing sick or disabled persons*, Prepared by IRS Research for the Health and Safety Executive and the Disability Rights Commission 2003

ment for those on IB and RB. We agree with the criticism that sheltered employment can isolate disabled people from the mainstream labour market and do little to advance the cause of disabled employment in the general workforce. Sheltered employment schemes in most countries tend to operate as an alternative to the mainstream labour market for those whose disabilities are too severe for them to have realistic prospects of entering mainstream employment. The strategy of offering short-term subsidies to employers combined with extended government support for adjusting mainstream workplaces is a better approach to promoting sustained increases in the employment level of sick and disabled people than sheltered employment.

3.5 Conditionality

The application of conditionality to current IB claimants relies heavily on the ability of our proposed testing system to distinguish between those with a work-inhibiting health condition who we can nonetheless reasonably expect to do some type of work in the future and those on whom we can place no such expectation; the former claiming a new Rehabilitation Benefit (RB), while the latter remain on IB (see section 3.1). Those on IB are those with the most severe disabilities who cannot be reasonably expected to work in the future, and there should accordingly be no job-search requirements placed upon them.

With regard to claimants of RB, however, having reached a judgement that they are people who we can reasonably expect to work in the future, we can immediately overcome one objection to job-search related conditionality – that it imposes unnecessary stress on those for whom a return to work is not a realistic prospect. By separating out the latter group onto IB, we can protect them from having excessive demands place upon them, while at the same time addressing the needs of those on RB who are closer to the labour market. Given the importance of maintaining a focus on a return to work, we would advocate making engagement with the rehabilitation and job-seeking process (set out in section 3.2) a condition of the receipt of RB.

In recognition of the time that rehabilitation may take, we would propose that there should be a period of six months during which time no specific job-seeking conditions are imposed on anyone claiming RB. At the end of this period, there will be a follow-up test, at which point a judgement is reached as to whether an individual can be expected to do certain types of work. For those who cannot be reasonably expected to take work of any sort but who remain on RB as opposed to IB (meaning that there is still a reasonable expectation of them working in the future), the same demands as before apply, namely that they engage with the rehabilitation process but without any specific job-seeking requirements. For those who can reasonably be expected to do work of some type, this should be recognised by making certain job-seeking demands of them. In addition to regular meetings with a Personal Adviser they should be limited in the offers of employment they can refuse. As with JSA claimants, there should be a limit of three jobs refused before sanctions can be applied. The sanctions should constitute benefit cuts of the same order of magnitude as are imposed on those JSA claimants who fail to meet their obligation to accept one of the first three reasonable job offers they receive.

Due to the different needs and levels of job-readiness among RB claimants, we do not propose being overly prescriptive regarding their obligations. Though the job-focused interviews are compulsory, there is no specific compulsion in the system beyond that with regard to complying with the Action Plan that is drawn up in the initial interview, itself tailored to the individual's needs. At the same time, however, the conditionality that arises after six months (or when the claimant is classed as capable of some work, whichever is the later) should prove sufficient incentive to participate in the rehabilitation programme. Likewise, given that only three reasonable job offers can be refused before sanctions are applied, this should provide an incentive for claimants to take job offers within the first six months where they are appropriate for them and their medical condition. The effectiveness of the conditions surrounding RB is reinforced by the fact that those who do take work but find themselves for medical reasons unable to continue with it are eligible to return to RB, with the additional support that entails (see section 3.3).

The approach to conditionality outlined above is one

embedded in the concept of individuals' rights and responsibilities that frames much of the current approach to other disadvantaged groups, such as the long-term unemployed. The distinction between those who can reasonably be expected to be able to work in the future and those on whom such an expectation cannot be placed can be seen as a distinction between those who are considered to have a duty to society to do what is necessary to return to work and those who do not have such a duty. At the same time, the state has a duty to those with illnesses or disabilities that prevent them from working to help rehabilitate them to be able to work and to ensure that they do not encounter discrimination in gaining or retaining employment on the basis of their disability (the latter extending to demanding the reasonable adjustments that form part of the Disability Discrimination Act).

SMF Publications

Whose Responsibility is it Anyway?
Jessica Asato (ed.)
This collection of essays brings together different perspectives
on the public health debate, seeking to find the balance
between state intervention and individual responsibility.
Published in the lead up to the second White Paper on public
health, it considers who should take responsibility for changing
public behaviour and when it is legitimate for the state
to intervene.
October 2004, £8.00

Reinventing Government Again
Liam Byrne and Philip Collins (eds.)
Ten years had passed since the publication of Osborne and
Gaebler's landmark book *Reinventing Government*. Thus, in
2004, the Social Market Foundation commissioned several
authors to reflect on the ten principles for entrepreneurial
government that were set out in the original.
December 2004, £15.00

Limits of the Market, Constraints of the State: The public good and the NHS
Rt. Hon Dr John Reid MP
In this essay, Dr. John Reid, then Secretary of State for Health,
lays out the case for extending patient choice within the NHS.
He tackles two misconceptions head-on: the belief that 'choice'
is a value solely for those on the ideological right; and the idea
that choice is only meaningful within markets where the
chooser's own private money is brought to bear.
January 2005, £10.00

Choice and Contestability in Primary Care
Social Market Foundation Health Commission Report 3
This paper examines the case for introducing certain kinds of
choice into the primary care sector of the NHS. It describes the
evolution of the current PCT structure of primary care and the
reasons for thinking that it is theoretically possible for PCTs to

improve the quality and cut the costs of service. It also presents the case for allowing GP practices to choose the PCT to which they wish to belong, explains how this system could operate in practice and considers the limitations of the system.
February 2005, £10.00

News Broadcasting in the Digital Age
Ann Rossiter
Rossiter argues for the introduction of 'genre' licences, providing commercial broadcasters with the opportunity to bid for financial support to provide specific public service broadcasting (PSB) programming, paid for by 'top-slicing' the BBC licence fee. She argues that the switch from analogue to digital broadcasting removes the incentive for commercial broadcasters to make and show PSB content, particularly at peak times.
February 2005, £10.00

The Future of Incapacity Benefit
Report of the Social Market Foundation Seminar
of December 2004
Moussa Haddad (ed.)
Figures produced in 2004 show that more than 50 percent of claimants have been on incapacity benefit for more than five years. Drawing on thoughts presented at an SMF seminar, Jane Kennedy, then Minister for Work at the Department for Work and Pensions, outlines the steps government is taking to combat the 'incapacity trap'.
February 2005, £10.00

Too Much, Too Late: Life chances and spending on education and training
Vidhya Alakeson
This report argues that the link between educational attainment and family background will not be broken as long as the pattern of spending on education and training continues to offer a far greater public subsidy to tertiary rather than preschool education. The report proposes a reallocation of spending in the medium term in favour of children under five.
March 2005, £15.00